Stanley Sharpleton was an amazing kid! First, he built his very own spaceship. Then, he took it for a little spin. He zoomed past Jupiter and Saturn and Pluto. In fact, he kept right on rocketing until he reached a far-off purple planet called Krimular.

1

Stanley slipped on his gravity-defying sneakers and hurried down the space ladder. He'd done it! He'd landed on planet Krimular and he couldn't wait to explore.

After walking a while, he reached a city. Aha! Just as he had suspected, there WAS life on Krimular! But something about this planet was very, very strange. Stanley just couldn't quite figure out what it was.

Suddenly Stanley felt a tap on his shoulder. He whirled around. "Greetings, Earthling," said a bright green creature with several arms. "Zik is named Zik. Tell Zik the name used to call the Earthling."

Stanley told Zik his name. "Zik is glad to meet Stanley," said Zik. "Stanley and Zik can be friends."

"Zik will show Stanley around Krimular," said Zik. "Look! Zik sees a Groogulak." Stanley looked where Zik pointed and saw a strange and beautiful animal. "Shhh," said Zik. "Stanley and Zik must not startle the Groogulak."

Speaking, reading, and writing would be a lot harder without pronouns. What do you know about this important group of little words? Share your ideas.

Suddenly, Stanley knew what was strange about Krimular. Zik didn't use pronouns. In fact, there were no pronouns to be found on the entire planet!

Stanley was happy to have met Zik. Without pronouns, though, it sure was going to be hard to communicate with his new friend. "Your planet is so amazing!" said Stanley. "But you could describe it even better if you used pronouns. Would you like to learn more about them?"

Important Pronouns

I		he	you
me	it	him	yours
mine	its	his	
			she
we		they	her
us		them	hers
ours		theirs	

A pronoun is a word that is used in place of a noun. Pronouns make sentences shorter and cut down on repetition.

When Zik nodded enthusiastically, Stanley pulled a collapsible space blackboard from his back pocket. "Pronouns are small words such as *I*, *you*, *me*, *her*, or *them*," explained Stanley. "They are used in place of nouns to make sentences simpler. Think of them as 'shortcut' words. For example, instead of saying, '*Zik* sees a *Groogulak*,' you could say, '*I* see *it*.'"

9

When the lesson was done, Zik said, "*I* have processed the concept of pronouns and will master *it* shortly."

"Boy, you learn quickly!" replied Stanley.

"Not only do *I* have six hands, *I* also have six brains," remarked Zik. "Now, let's tour the rest of the planet."

You can use the pronoun *it* in place of long words, like *ballcano*, to make sentences neater.

Zik showed Stanley a huge volcano that spewed pink and green smoke and big bouncy balls with fancy patterns. "Take a look at the ballcano," said Zik. "The ballcano erupts every day. Correction: *It* erupts every day. *I* got so excited that *I* almost forgot to use pronouns."

Some pronouns are used in place of people's names. These include *I*, *you*, *he*, and *she*.

Just then it started to snow, even though the weather was very warm. Zik darted about, catching the flakes in his mouth. "Zik loves snow. Correction: *I* love snow! Gee, pronouns do make things easier!"

Some pronouns are used to show ownership. These include *mine*, *your*, *yours*, *his*, *her*, *ours*, *theirs*, and *its*.

Stanley caught a flake on his tongue. It tasted like watermelon. He caught another. It tasted like a hot dog. He caught another. It tasted like pizza. "This one is the best!" he said.

Zik then replied, "Stanley's favorite flavor is pizza and so is Zik's. Correction: *Your* favorite flavor is pizza and so is *mine*."

At last, it was time for Stanley to return to Earth. "Thanks for teaching *me* all about pronouns. *They* sure come in handy," said Zik.

"Thanks for showing me all around Krimular. It's really out of this world!" exclaimed Stanley.

Next, Stanley gave Zik a farewell gift. It was his latest invention, an intergalactic cell phone. "This will help us keep in touch," he said.

"Wow! Thanks Stanley," replied Zik. "Correction: Thank *you*! *I* like *it* almost as much as *I* like pronouns."

Go on a pronoun hunt!
How many can you find
in this story? When
you're done, talk about
everything you learned.

Back on Earth, Stanley got a call from Zik. "Is *it* all right if my family and *I* come for a visit?" he asked.

"Sure. You can stay in our guest room," said Stanley.

"Perfect," responded Zik. "Expect *us* Thursday—*me*, my parents, and my 2,978 brothers and sisters. *I* told *them* all about pronouns and *they* each want a lesson!"